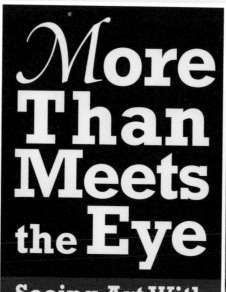

More Than Meets the Eye

Seeing Art With All Five Senses

Bob Raczka

M̱ Millbrook Press ◆ Minneapolis

Millbrook Press
A division of Lerner Publishing Group, Inc.
241 First Avenue North
Minneapolis, MN 55401 U.S.A.

Website address: www.lernerbooks.com

Library of Congress Cataloging-in-Publication Data

Raczka, Bob.
    More than meets the eye : seeing art with all five senses / by Bob
Raczka.
        p.   cm.
    Summary: Provides images of paintings and new, sensory ways to
experience them, such as tasting the milk in Vermeer's "The Milkmaid,"
hearing the music in Tanner's "The Banjo Lesson," or feeling the fur in
da Vinci's "Lady with an Ermine."
    ISBN-13: 978–0–7613–2797–4 (lib. bdg. : alk. paper)
    ISBN-10: 0–7613–2797–5 (lib. bdg. : alk. paper)
    ISBN-13: 978–0–7613–1994–8 (pbk. : alk. paper)
    ISBN-10: 0–7613–1994–8 (pbk. : alk. paper)
    1. Painting—Appreciation—Juvenile literature. 2. Art
appreciation—Juvenile literature. [1. Painting. 2. Art appreciation.]
    1. Title.
NDII43.R33 2003
759—dc21   2003000343

Manufactured in the United States of America
5 – DP – 12/1/09

If you've ever been to an art museum or an art show at your school, you know how much fun it is to look at paintings. But have you ever **tasted** a painting?

Bite an apple

Apples in a Tin Pail

Levi Wells Prentice ◆ 1892 ◆ Museum of Fine Arts, Boston

Drink some milk

The Kitchen Maid

Jan Vermeer ◆ c. 1658-60 ◆ Rijksmuseum, Amsterdam

Sip a cup of tea

The Tea

Mary Cassatt ◆ 1880 ◆ Museum of Fine Arts, Boston

Eat a piece of frosted cake

Cakes

Wayne Thiebaud ♦ 1963 ♦ National Gallery of Art, Washington, D.C.

Or lobster from the sea.

Still Life with Lobster, Drinking Horn, and Glasses

Willem Kalf ♦ c. 1653 ♦ National Gallery, London

Now that you've tested your artistic taste buds, see what you can **hear** when you listen to a painting.

Cannons boom

Capture of H.B.M. Frigate Macedonian by
U.S. Frigate United States, October 25, 1812

Thomas Chambers ◆ 1852 ◆ Smithsonian American Art Museum, Washington, D.C.

Fingers pluck

The Banjo Lesson

Henry Ossawa Tanner ◆ 1893 ◆ Hampton University Museum, Hampton, Virginia

Diver makes a splash

A Bigger Splash

David Hockney ◆ 1967 ◆ Tate Gallery, London

Paddles thwack
two rubber balls

The Bo-Lo Game

Jacob Lawrence ◆ 1937 ◆ The Newark Museum, Newark, New Jersey

Fencing foils clash.

The Fencers

Milton Avery • 1944 • Santa Barbara Museum of Art, Santa Barbara, California

Okay, you've tasted some paintings and listened to some paintings. Are you ready to **smell** a few?

Stinky pig

Portrait of Pig

James Wyeth • 1970 • Brandywine River Museum, Chadds Ford, Pennsylvania

Fragrant flowers

Flower Piece

Rachel Ruysch ◆ c. 1690 ◆ Cheltenham Art Museums, Cheltenham, England

Baby's breath so sweet

The Cradle

Berthe Morisot ◆ 1872 ◆ Musée d'Orsay, Paris

Three old pairs of smelly shoes

Three Pairs of Shoes

Vincent van Gogh ◆ 1886–1887 ◆ Fogg Art Museum, Harvard University Art Museums, Cambridge, Massachusetts

Fresh-cut stacks of wheat.

Stacks of Wheat (End of Summer)

Claude Monet ◆ 1890-91 ◆ The Art Institute of Chicago, Chicago, Illinois

Pat tortillas

The Tortilla Maker

Diego Rivera ✦ 1926 ✦ University of California, San Francisco

Hold a hand

A Dancing Couple

Gerard Terborch ◆ 1660 ◆ National Trust, Polesden Lacey, Dorking, Sussex, England

Stroke an ermine's coat

Lady with an Ermine

Leonardo da Vinci ◆ 1483-90 ◆ Czartoryski Museum, Kraków

Catch the wind

Sun and Wind on the Roof

John Sloan ◆ 1915 ◆ Maier Museum of Art at Randolph-Macon Woman's College, Lynchburg, Virginia

Or find out
what it feels like to float.

Birthday

Marc Chagall • 1915 • The Museum of Modern Art, New York

Of course, enjoying art starts with looking. Here are some paintings that are just plain fun to **look** at.

Count the pictures

The Archduke Leopold's Gallery

David Teniers the Younger ◆ 1651 ◆ Kunsthistorischas Museum, Vienna, Austria

Find the skull

(Hint: Tilt the book flat and look at the picture from the bottom left-hand corner.)

The Ambassadors

Hans Holbein the Younger ◆ 1533 ◆ National Gallery, London

See what makes art tick

Watch

Gerald Murphy ◆ 1925 ◆ Dallas Museum of Art, Dallas, Texas

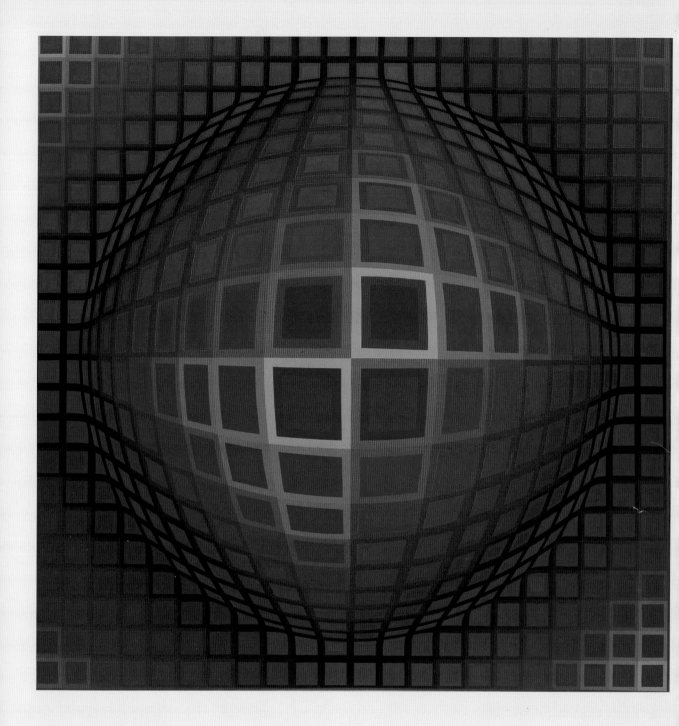

View a circle made of squares

Vega-Nor

Victor Vasarely ♦ 1969 ♦ Albright-Knox Art Gallery, Buffalo, New York

Or let your eyes be tricked.

(Hint: Look closely at the face to see what it's made of.)

Self-Portrait

Chuck Close ◆ 2000 ◆ Pace Prints, New York

> **Once you've used all your senses to enjoy art, you'll never just look at a painting again!**

About the Artists

Milton Avery (1885–1965) American abstract painter, known for his use of muted colors and simplified shapes.

Mary Cassatt (1844–1926) American Impressionist painter who spent much of her life in Paris; known best for her pictures of mothers and their children.

Marc Chagall (1887–1985) French painter and designer, born in Russia, known for his poetically surrealistic paintings and images of fantasy.

Thomas Chambers (1808–1866 or after) American painter of landscapes and marine scenes; born in London.

Chuck Close (1940–   ) American painter, specializes in photo-realistic portraits using different types of grids.

Vincent van Gogh (1853–1890) Dutch Expressionist painter, known for his use of vivid colors and bold brushstrokes.

David Hockney (1937–   ) British painter of portraits and landscapes who works mainly in America; also known for his photo collages.

Hans Holbein the Younger (1497?–1543) German portrait painter, known for his realistic and forceful likenesses; became court painter to King Henry VIII.

Willem Kalf (1619–1693) Dutch still-life painter who specialized in detailed pictures of fruit and precious objects.

Jacob Lawrence (1917–2000) African American painter, part of the Harlem Renaissance, known for his narrative paintings of African American life.

Leonardo da Vinci (1452–1519) Italian painter, sculptor, architect, scientist, and inventor; best known for his intelligence and interest in just about everything.

Claude Monet (1840–1926) French painter, a leader of the Impressionist movement, who was interested in the effects of outdoor light and atmosphere.

 Berthe Morisot (1841–1895) French Impressionist painter, known for paintings of women and children; often used members of her own family as models.

 Gerald Murphy (1888–1964) American painter, specialized in painting everyday objects in flat colors; produced only a handful of finished works.

 Levi Wells Prentice (1851–1935) American still-life painter; also did portraits and landscapes; self-taught.

 Diego Rivera (1886–1957) Mexican painter, influenced by indigenous art, known for his large murals portraying the history and social problems of Mexico.

 Rachel Ruysch (1664–1750) Dutch still-life painter who specialized in intricate flower pieces.

 John Sloan (1871–1951) American painter and illustrator, a member of the "Ashcan School," known for his paintings of life in the city.

 Henry Ossawa Tanner (1859–1937) African American painter who specialized in scenes of African American life and biblical subjects; moved to Paris to escape racial prejudice.

 David Teniers the Younger (1610–1690) Dutch painter who left behind more than 2,000 works; known best for scenes of peasant life.

 Gerard Terborch (1617–1681) Dutch painter who specialized in full-length portraits and simplified interior scenes.

 Wayne Thiebaud (1920–) American painter of still-lifes, portraits, and landscapes; best known for his paintings of pies and desserts.

 Victor Vasarely (1908–1997) French painter, widely regarded as the father of Op Art, his motto was "Art for All."

 Jan Vermeer (1632–1675) Dutch painter who specialized in interior scenes of everyday life; known for his ability to paint light.

 James Wyeth (1946–) Third-generation American realist painter; subjects include portraits, animals, and architecture.